Rainforest Biome

Mediterranean Biome

Outdoor Biome

Core

Stage

Link

Biome entrance

Visitor Centre

SkyWire

Pineapple car park

0.26

0.25 →

0.01 — 0.26

The Eden Project is an educational charity. Eden creates gardens, exhibitions, art, events, experiences and projects that explore how people can work together and with nature to change things for the better.

D1459118

Contents

Welcome to our Living Theatre of Plants and People.

This guide gives a flavour of the sort of things we do. Come on in, explore our exhibits, take part in our events and have a chat with the team.

To keep in touch follow us online, become a Friend and/or get involved in some of our projects.

Planning your day   6

Your tour guide

The Outdoor Biome   8

The Core   18

The Rainforest Biome   22

The Mediterranean Biome   32

Eden Live: seasonal events   40

Eden – the back story   42

Eden's projects   54

Where has the money come from?   58

What can we do?   60

Biome maps   64

What is Eden about?

1999

The Eden Project, an educational charity, creates gardens, exhibitions, art, events, experiences and projects that explore how people can work together and with nature to change things for the better. Our first project was to make a 35-acre global garden in a 50m-deep crater that was once a china clay pit to demonstrate regeneration and the art of the possible.

2003

The Living Theatre of Plants and People

We called our HQ the Living Theatre of Plants and People because in it we celebrate our relationship with and dependence on plants: plants that feed us, clothe us, cure us, make and colour our fabrics and our lives and even supply the very air we breathe.

The Visitor Centre serves as the beginning and end of your visit. It looks out over the two vast covered Biomes which house wild landscapes, crops and stories from the Rainforest and Mediterranean regions. These bubble-shaped greenhouses serve as a backdrop to our Outdoor Biome (the one without the roof), which grows the plants from our own climate. The Link connects all three Biomes together and takes plant to plate with a range of delicious foods in the Eden Kitchen. The Core, with the spiky roof, gets to the core of the issue, brings the threads of the story together in a range of exhibits and exhibitions and shows the work of many of Eden's projects. Across the site there are many places to eat, rest and play (and masses of loos too). Take a look at the **Planning your day** page overleaf and the maps on the inside covers, and have a chat to any of our team who will help you find things that would best interest you.

Why plants?

Plants are our lifeblood. The natural world is our life-support system. Each of our Biomes is divided into two main areas: the wild landscapes and the cropped areas.

Wild landscapes

Plants provide services.

Worldwide, plant ecosystems regulate our climate, provide the oxygen for us to breathe, purify water, make clouds, make soil and recycle waste.

Plant leaves are the original solar panels. They capture the energy from the sun and combine it with water and carbon dioxide to make a type of sugar that all living things can then use as a source of energy and a building block for everything.

Plants also provide inspiration for design, and generally help us feel good. At Eden we bring you wild landscapes from the American prairies to the largest rainforest in captivity.

Crops

Plants provide resources.

From coffee beans to blue jeans, we use plants for everything: foods, fuels, medicines, fabrics, building materials, musical instruments, sports equipment, transport, makeup, books, furniture, drinks, entertainment ... You name it, they are usually in there somewhere.

Even oil, petrol, coal and plastics have their origins in the plants of the seas and our great primeval forests.

Plants inhabit every part of our lives including our dreams, myths and stories.

People grow crops and harvest from the wild to feed our needs.

Our exhibits explore the plant-people stories that reconnect us all to our world, to encourage us to care about it, because it's amazing and because it keeps us alive. It's also a shot over our bows: what we do to nature we do to ourselves. We need to crop the land and conserve the wild places.

Wild landscapes   Crops

And people?

We need to live in balance with this natural world to overcome some of the challenges we have imposed on it.

As Douglas Adams (of *Hitchhiker's Guide to the Galaxy* fame) said: 'The world is big enough to look after itself. What we have to be concerned about is whether or not the world we live in will be capable of sustaining us in it.'

We are inspired by the belief that people are more than capable of changing things for the better. In the last few years we have learnt what hope, faith, ingenuity, resourcefulness and determination can do. As time goes by we are able to show more and more new ways of doing things in the 21st century. You will find the stories across the site.

So travel the world in a day, explore the exhibits, trek through the world's largest rainforest in captivity, meander through the Med, enjoy events and concerts, trace plants to plates and eat delicious foods all prepared with the planet in mind.

The Plant Takeaway – *aka Dead Cat, Visitor Centre.*
Discover what happens when the plants we use are taken away. Follow the adventures of Alan, Enid, Sniff the cat and Digger the dog in the children's guidebook.

5

Planning your day

Covered Biome Entrance

Rainforest Biome

Stage

Link

Land Train

Outdoor Biome

Rainforest Biome

The largest rainforest in captivity. Trek through the steamy jungle, discover how rainforests keep us alive and how we can help do the same for them. Bananas? Coffee? Cashews? All here. Explore the need for a balance between the world's wild places and the cropped land-scapes. Visit our new Rainforest Canopy Walkway and take a walk in the treetops.

(II) **Baobab Smoothie Bar open when possible.**

Land Train

Every 15–20 minutes between Visitor Centre and Stage area.

Stage

The base for our seasonal events programme: Freaky Nature, Eden Sessions (music events), summer family activities and barbecues, Harvest, Halloweden and our winter festival. See **edenproject.com**.

(II) **Great food in and around the Stage when there's an event on.**

Outdoor Biome

Back in 1998 this Biome (with the sky for a roof) was a barren landscape, with no soil and no plants. Today it celebrates our dependence on plants, presents our cropped and wild landscapes and explores their importance.

Link

This grass-roofed building serves as the entrance to both covered Biomes and the Eden Kitchen. There are also loads of loos, our little shop and membership desks.

(II) **Eden Kitchen. Tasty food prepared and cooked in front of your eyes. Join us round our kitchen table.**

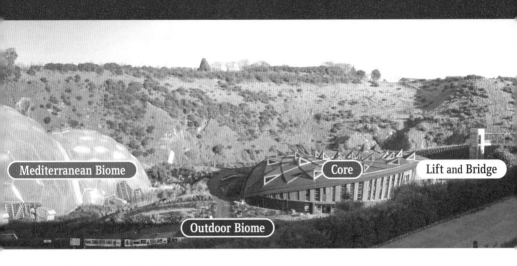

Mediterranean Biome

Core

Outdoor Biome

Lift and Bridge

Mediterranean Biome

Sights, scents and stories from the Mediterranean, South Africa and California. Visit the wild landscapes and stroll through the world's kitchen gardens – wild vines, age-old olives, the citrus grove; we need both, it's all a matter of balance.

🍴 **Eden Med Terrace. Authentic delicious Mediterranean food. Get in that holiday mood.**

Lift and Bridge join The Core and Visitor Centre.

Core

Home to exhibitions, films, art, play, schools workshops, the giant Seed sculpture and the world's largest nutcracker. Explore global challenges and some solutions.

🍴 **The Core Café. Open in the busy seasons for baguettes, soups, salads and platters.**

Visitor Centre

The way in and out, tickets, membership desks, our big shop, plant sales, ATM and loos.

🍴 **The Eden Coffee House, a pit stop on arrival or departure – sandwiches, soups, cakes, coffee...**

Food

🍴 The food we serve reflects the stories we tell. It is responsibly sourced: fairly-traded, direct-sourced, organic, seasonal, and/or local and freshly made. We cater for vegetarians, vegans, meat-eaters and gluten-free diets. There are several cafés to choose from. Check site for opening times. Some cafes close in quieter periods.

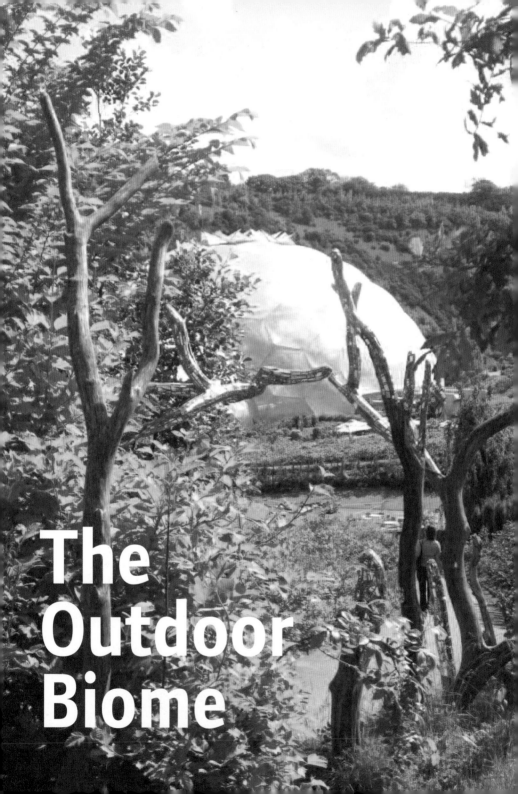

The Outdoor Biome

The Outdoor Biome

Taking it from the top

Welcome to the Outdoor Biome 0.01

You can get a great overview of the site from the platform outside the Visitor Centre and further down to the left at the Junction. In our Outdoor Biome there are over twenty exhibits exploring the crops and wild landscapes of our own climate (list and map inside front cover). The entrance to the covered Biomes is in the grass-covered Link building between them.

Zigzag area

Flowerless garden 0.02

Journey through plant evolution, from the earliest mosses to the bryophytes, ferns and horsetails that grew in hot, steamy conditions over 350 million years ago, before the dinosaurs. They created coal as they rotted. Burning it releases the CO_2 they locked up and is heating up the planet again. (More about climate change in the Core.) Also look out for the planet's first flowering plants, Magnolia and Drimys, and the Wollemi pine, one of the world's rarest and oldest plants.

WEEEman 0.03

Our waste giant is made from all the Waste Electrical and Electronic Equipment (about 3.3 tonnes) one person throws away in a lifetime. Designed by Paul Bonomini.

2002

Crops that feed the world   0.04

Three plant species – wheat, maize and rice – feed most of the world. They provide carbohydrates and some protein, and store well. Other major staples include potatoes, beans and bananas. Rapid world population growth led to wheat and rice breeding programmes in the 1960s and 70s to increase crop yields. This 'Green Revolution' staved off predicted large-scale starvation.

Wheat for...	Maize for...	Rice for...
Bread	Corn on the cob	Rice (steamed, fried, etc)
Cakes, biscuits	Cornflakes	Rice Krispies
Pasta	Tortillas	Risotto
Wheat noodles	Animal food	Rice cakes
Animal food	Popcorn	Rice pudding

Today's challenges include a growing population (over 7 billion, possibly growing to 10.5 billion by 2050); inequity in distribution; over-consumption and cheap food in many developed countries and hunger in many developing countries; a lack of reserves; rising oil prices; the food/fuel debate (see exhibit 0.12); land grabs; price hikes and climate change. Possible solutions include increasing yields and soil fertility, pest and disease resistance, biotechnology, agricultural biodiversity, new crops that can cope with the changing climate, trade justice, conflict resolution, poverty alleviation, good nutrition projects and education. On a personal level, think about what we eat and where it comes from, waste less, eat less meat (60% of maize production is used as animal feed) and grow your own.

The Garden of Senses 0.05

There are around 500,000 hectares of gardens in the UK (twice the area of nature reserves). Our own gardens represent a personal connection to nature, serving all sorts of purposes.

A Sense of Memory

Inspired by memories of childhood Cornish holidays, this garden was created by Thomas Hoblyn, for the RHS Chelsea Flower Show 2011. Thanks to Tom and Homebase, it was given a permanent home at Eden. Send us your fond memories of particular plants and we'll put them online. **edenproject/memories**.

A Sense of History

Garden flowers have their origins in wild places across the world. Favourites were bred to produce the garden varieties we are familiar with today. The dahlia originated in Central America; stems of its ancestors were once used as water pipes.

A Sense of Place

This social garden has the environment close to its heart. Drought-resistant plants were chosen to avoid watering, and paths made from local materials to avoid air miles.

A Sense of Play

Our play garden is made of willow and wood, helping to reconnect children with nature. Tip: push pieces of willow in and they take root, weave it into any shape you want. More tips on the website.

A Sense of Taste

A productive garden half this size can provide a family of four with fresh veg all year round. If you are short of space just grow your favourites. Rocket takes only five to six weeks from sowing to eating.

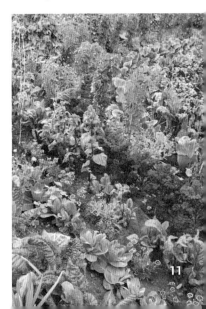

A Sense of Scents

Herbs, most of which don't need much water, are perfect for growing in pots. You know it makes scents.

A Sense of Colour

A range of borders with themed colours: red, white and blue creating a stunning impact. Planting schemes are available from our plant shop and **edenproject.com**.

Stage area

The Hive in the Orchard 0.06

In our Hive building enjoy films and/or seasonal workshops. (NB The Hive is occasionally closed for private functions)

Orchards: a place of relaxation and, in autumn, fast food (in a biodegradable wrapper). Only around 11% of our annual fruit consumption is produced in the UK, but interest in health and local produce means that orchards are making a comeback. Try growing some tasty old varieties, start a community orchard near you, have an apple day. You can try some Cornish apple juice in our shop.

Pollination 0.07

Plants can't move (much). Many reproduce by luring insects and other animals to take their pollen from flower to flower. Insect/flower relationships are often very specific. Over a third of our food plants worldwide depend on pollinators – let's look after them.

Lavender, from the Latin *lavare* ('to wash'), cleans and calms. It is used in aromatherapy oils, perfumes, insect repellents and antiseptics. Bees love it too and make delicious honey from it.

Cornish crops 0.08

Cornwall's mild climate means that it can supply the UK with early crops and quality foods year round. Eden food uses local produce wherever possible.

Beer and brewing 0.09

Look out for beer ingredients (barley and hops), the hop stilt walker, the brewing kettle and the isinglass (tropical catfish swim bladder) used to clear beer, on our hop poles.

Tea 0.10

Made from the young leaves of the tea bush, *Camellia sinensis*, tea grows in the subtropics, as well as the cool, moist, more mountainous tropics – and in Cornwall!

Global gardens 0.11

Discover new veg to grow in your garden, from gardening communities with roots in Africa, Asia, Latin America, the Caribbean and Europe. Find out more about Eden's Gardens for Life project: a global network of schools that explore the world through gardening and growing food. **edenproject.com/gardens-for-life**.

Crops for a material world O.12

Plants can be grown for fibres, fuels and even plastics.

Industrial hemp provides food and health products, clothing, car components and building materials with a lower carbon footprint than concrete. Hemp grows well in the UK, needing few agro-chemicals (cotton uses around 25% of the world's pesticides). Legally we have to have a barrier round our hemp crop, so George Fairhurst designed us a hemp fence. He made our Metal Giant too. Give the rope a tug to see how strong plant fibres are.

Sunflowers provide high-quality oils for lubrication, plastic manufacture and biodiesel as well as food. Plant sugars and starch from maize and wheat make bioethanol for fuel and compostable plastic cutlery, carrier bags, nappies, etc. Plants grown for biofuels are having their carbon footprint scrutinised, and the food-versus-fuel debate means a search for alternative raw materials. Biomass to Liquids (BTL) factories can turn waste straw, wood waste, stalks, etc, into fuel, even biokerosene to power aircraft.

West side

Prairie 0.13

Looks great in full flower in August. The American prairies were partially created by man, using controlled burning to attract game (to young post-fire grass) and ease travelling. They once covered a quarter of the US. In some areas, up to 99% have been destroyed in the last 150 years. Work is underway to conserve these diverse grasslands and let the buffalo roam once more. Why conserve? Provision of ecosystem services (see the Core, p.21), climate control and potential future crops for starters. We manage our own prairie by burning in Jan/Feb, then the plants start to come through: Camassias, Liatris, Echinaceas *(right)* … Some public parks are now turning to prairie-style plantings: better for biodiversity, cheaper and easier to maintain than bedding.

Plants for a changing climate 0.14

Our extreme gardeners explore adaptation and try new plants in tricky situations.

Biomass fuels 0.15

David Kemp's 'Industrial Plant' sculpture and his 'Greenhouse of New Worlds' take a sideways look at fossil fuels, which currently provide around 85% of the world's energy. The developed world (16% of the world's population) uses 53% of this energy, while nearly half the world's people (mainly in developing countries) rely on wood, charcoal and dung, which have a low carbon footprint: the amount of CO_2 absorbed during their growth equals the amount emitted on burning. Willow, poplar and miscanthus are burnt for biomass in the UK. Other energy choices include wind and water power, algae as fuel, solar and nuclear power and geothermal, using heat from the earth.

Myth and folklore 0.16

Stories keep plants alive in our memory, and our storytellers bring you tales across the site. Pete Hill and Kate Munro created our willow Dream Chamber. Its classic seven-ring labyrinth is found worldwide. To sailors it was a good-luck token, ensuring safe return. It provided protection against wandering spirits who get lost in the curves (spirits can only travel in straight lines, allegedly).

Wild Cornwall 0.17

Cornwall's biodiversity, its varied landscapes, habitats and wildlife, has been shaped by its climate, geology, geography and people. Heathlands are partly man-made; they started forming 6,000 to 3,500 years ago when woodland was cleared for hunting and agriculture, and need managing to prevent them reverting. Since 1800 Cornwall has lost over 90% of its lowland heath. Conservationists in Cornwall are helping to restore, protect and manage what is left. In Cornwall 75% of the land is farmed, though farming also provides rich habitats. Here, sculptors Peter Martin and Sarah Stewart-Smith have immortalised rare Cornish species in stone, and Chris Drury created the Cloud Chamber.

Mining the earth: metals, minerals and energy 0.18

We're as dependent on mining as we are on agriculture. Eden is a world-class example of how an old mine site can be reclaimed when the mine has reached the end of its useful life (in mining terms). Turn the giant wheel to discover the story of the copper on the Core roof: responsibly sourced from a single mine. Climb into the mini tunnel to discover underground secrets and how the mining industry is working towards good practice and responsible mining.

Core side

Health 0.19

Half the herbs sold worldwide are wild-harvested, which done responsibly can sustain environments and livelihoods. Herbs and pharmaceuticals (e.g. morphine from opium poppies) are also grown as crops. With 'pharming', crops are modified and used as biological factories to produce drugs: pills from plants!

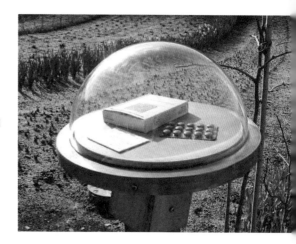

Dyes 0.20

Woad and indigo give us blue, weld yellow and madder red. Indigo-dyed cloth comes out of the dye vat yellow and turns blue as it oxidises in the air.

Paper 0.21

Plants growing here can be made into paper. Many natural habitats have been cleared and planted with Eucalyptus and *Pinus radiata* for paper-making. Agricultural residues containing cellulose, such as wheat and rice straw, can be used instead of wood pulp. World paper consumption is rocketing – so is recycling, luckily. Look out for the secret paths through the tall grasses.

The Spiral Garden 0.22

Making a school or community garden? Discover some low-cost ideas *(right)*: willow spirals, rainbows of flowers, soft paths, textured plants and scented plants.

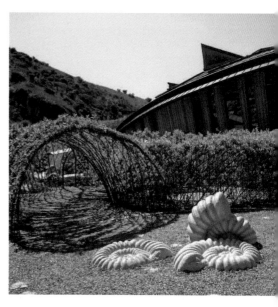

Timber 0.23

The plant labels are made from the timber they describe. Wood is a carbon store and timber construction is on the rise. Good for wood.

The Bluff 0.24

A place for picnics and play for children of all ages.

Fly across Eden on SkyWire, the longest zip wire in England. Access from Pineapple car park.

For cost, restrictions and opening times see edenproject.com/adventure

Book online, in the Visitor Centre, and at the SkyWire shed in Pineapple car park.

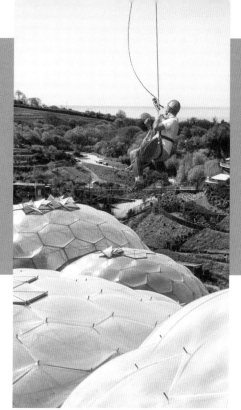

Outer estate

Forest garden 0.25

On your way down to or back from the Visitor Centre, explore our growing Forest Garden – full of useful wild plants for food, shelter and medicines.

Wild Chile 0.26

Behind Pineapple car park take a trip to Chile and explore our forest of beautiful plants. Central Chile is under threat from logging, agriculture and replacement with non-native pine and eucalyptus for paper and wood chip. This 'Safe Site' contains and protects wild-collected material from the Valdivian forests of central Chile, like this Embothrium – a living example of *ex-situ* conservation.

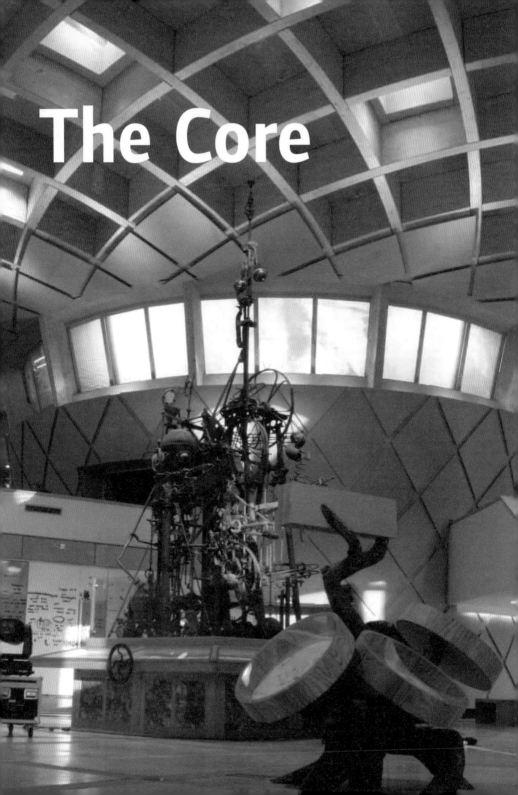

The Core

The Core

Eden's education, arts and events hub

The building itself is an exhibit. Its structure is based on a sunflower, which isn't one flower but hundreds which work together to create something better together. Eden's projects, many of which are described in the Core, also show what can be achieved by working together. The Seed, a 75-tonne sculpture carved from Cornish granite by Peter Randall Page, carries nature's pattern into the heart of the building and plants a symbol of hope, to grow ideas for the 21st century.

The pattern was inspired by the growth blueprint of plants, opposing spirals based on Fibonacci's sequence: 0, 1, 1, 2, 3, 5, 8, 13, 21, 34 ... where every number is the sum of the previous two. The spirals on a pinecone, pineapple and sunflower, like our roof, often exhibit two consecutive numbers in this sequence.

The Core building

The brief Fit for purpose, future-proof, made with responsibly sourced materials, energy efficient, with minimal waste. Grimshaws, who designed the covered Biomes, played another blinder, helped immeasurably by funding from the Millennium Commission, the South West Regional Development Agency and Cornwall's Objective One Programme.

The structure Double-curved glulam (glued laminated) timber beams, Swiss Forestry Stewardship Council endorsed.

The roof 40% of the world's copper is recycled. What about the other 60%, we wondered? Because of the way the market operates, it can be almost impossible for the end user to ensure that metals are responsibly produced and sourced. We traced the supply chain of the copper for our roof from a single Rio Tinto mine, known for its high environmental and social standards, all the way to Eden. This unusual initiative has led to much more work on the minerals supply chain.

Accessibility The Core is on three floors, and built into the landscape so that each one is accessible from ground level.

Floors You'll find recycled wood, plant-based floorings (Marmoleum from flax, carpets from maize), and concrete from china-clay sand (low carbon footprint). The little green tiles are made from recycled Heineken bottles.

Art Art is an integral part of the building. The Core and the Seed were designed together from the outset. In our solar terrace windows on the second floor Susan Derges created a beautiful array of photograms to represent the water cycle. The images were created on dark, starless nights by taking huge pieces of photographic film, immersing them in streams, rivers and the sea, exposing them to a flashlight for a second to imprint the image on to film, quickly putting the film into black bags to prevent further exposure, sending them for processing, printing and putting between two pieces of glass. The result: transient images immortalised.

The Core exhibits

Ground floor The huge glass ball, the Plant Engine, represents the world's wild landscapes - aka the ecosystems: rainforests, oceans, grasslands, etc. It breathes life into the bell jars containing automata which represent the 'ecosystem services' that keep us alive: regulating our climate, providing oxygen for us to breathe, purifying water, making clouds, making soil, recycling waste, providing inspiration for design, and generally helping us feel good.

Three challenges we impose on these systems – climate change, clean water provision, biodiversity loss – are explored in the little greenhouse, water tank and diversity cabinet, along with some solutions.

Biodiversity

Life in all its richness and variety. Nature is important, we're part of it and it keeps us alive. Human impact is causing many species to disappear, and with them the patterns of life and the processes that our lives, economies and societies depend on. Biodiversity loss is an issue, because if it goes too far we will be among its first victims.

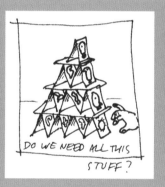

DO WE NEED ALL THIS STUFF?

A series of carts representing Eden's projects can be found throughout the building. More on our projects on p.54.

First floor

The Mezzanine: a seasonal programme of temporary exhibitions

Film Room: the Eden film interspersed with films from people we work with

Classrooms: for our schools programmes and events

Second floor

The Core Café: delicious food (closed on quieter days, but plenty to eat in the Eden Kitchen in the Link between the covered Biomes).

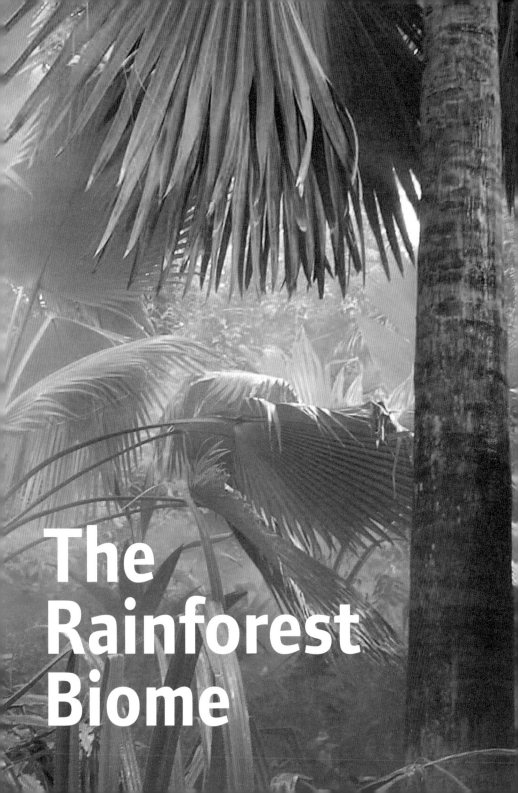

The Rainforest Biome

The Rainforest Biome

> 'Rainforest is the glue that holds the climate of our planet together. Lose the forest and it will have devastating consequences for all life on Earth.'
>
> Professor Sir Ghillean Prance, FRS

Welcome to the Rainforest Biome R.01

The Humid Tropic Regions are located between the Tropics of Cancer and Capricorn, 23.5° N and S of the Equator. Temperatures average 25°C all year round (5°C variation), with over 90% humidity and 1,500mm (60") annual rainfall. We've recreated these conditions here (except we do the watering before you arrive!) and in the last 14 years have grown the largest rainforest in captivity. Why?

The majestic rainforests that circle the globe are the planet's life-support system. We can't all go there; we decided to grow some here and together explore their secrets, discover how they keep us alive, learn of the challenges and, most important, share ways of trying to save them. On your Eden journey you can trek through four of the world's rainforests. The plants in each area may be different species but they have evolved to look similar to thrive in the climatic conditions. This year the first phase of our new Rainforest Canopy Walkway takes you into the treetops to explore the biodiversity close up.

Millions of people live in and make their living from the rainforests; we bring you some of their stories. You'll notice half the Biome grows crops: chocolate, coffee, spices, rubber, medicines... Traditionally forest was felled to cultivate some of these things. We explore the search for balance: finding ways to grow crops to meet people's needs (supporting livelihoods as well as providing consumer goods) whilst conserving the forest that keeps us all alive.

How does the rainforest keep us alive?

- Rainforests help regulate the earth's climate. They absorb and store CO_2 in their wood. They make a lot of rain too.
- They are also a huge store of biodiversity. Rainforests cover 5% of the earth's land mass and are home to half the world's terrestrial animal and plant species. Some have been used to keep us fed, clothed and cured. Many have still to be studied.
- And the forests produce oxygen (but not as much as do the algae in the sea).

An area of primary forest the size of this Biome is cut down every 10 seconds. Don't panic (yet); rainforests can regrow. There are many things we can do too – read on!

Explore the world's rainforests

Tropical islands: conserving the land R.02

Mangrove swamps protect the coast (e.g. against tsunamis), provide fuel, timber and a habitat for fish. Island habitats are home to many unusual, unique species. Climate change, invasive species, human settlement and tourism pose serious threats. Isolated island communities lack resources to conserve biodiversity, though conservation programmes offer hope: the rare Seychelles Coco-de-Mer, with huge seeds *(right)* that look like giant bottoms, was over-harvested (as trophies and perceived aphrodisiacs). Now each seed is registered and protected. Ours (a gift from the Seychelles) germinated five years after planting: one of very few specimens in the UK, it grows slowly – a leaf a year.

Southeast Asia: Orang dan Kebun (people and garden) R.03

Our traditional Malaysian home garden provides food year-round. Herbs and flowers nearest the house, vegetables, fruit and other useful trees further out. Winged beans replace our runner beans; both fertilise the soil. Pak choi, taro and rice replace cabbage, carrots and potatoes.

The garden also provides building materials, medicines and produce to barter or sell at local markets. The miracle tree, *Moringa oleifera*, has edible leaves, beans, flowers and roots. Its seeds are used as water filters and its oils for watchmaking.

To the left of the path is a rice paddy. In Asia 'rice is life', culturally and spiritually crucial to people's lives.

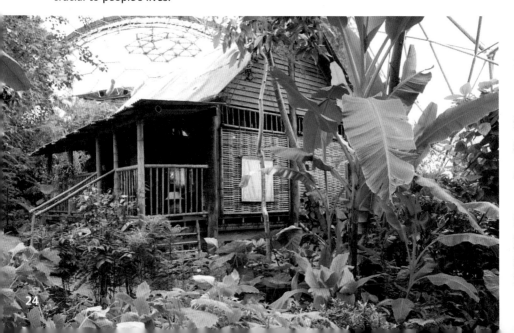

West Africa: managing the land R.04

The totems, by West African sculptor El Anatsui, came from charred timbers recycled from a part of Falmouth docks which was destroyed by fire. They started their life as trees in West Africa.

On your right, the forest has been partially cleared and selected trees left to provide fruits, spices and medicines. Further round, the chop farm, where areas of forest are cleared, grows light-loving crops such as groundnuts, cassava, rice, millet and traditional African leafy vegetables alongside pawpaw and bananas. Reverting to traditional crops in these areas rather than high-status Western crops helps provide a balanced diet and an income from local markets.

Our bantaba meeting place was created with help from the Ballabu Conservation Project, which hopes to create sustainable projects in and around 14 Gambian villages. We've a Gardens for Life project there too.

Tropical South America: shamanic art and cassava production R.06

Past the entrance to the new Rainforest Canopy Walkway (described overleaf) take the steep and stepped high road past the waterfall for a great panoramic view and see the work of Peruvian shamanic artists Montes Shuna and Panduro Baneo, showing a spiritual connection between plants and people. The flat low road takes you past the tallest tree in the Biome (the kapok).

The paths meet near a clearing where a hut shows the processing of cassava into tapioca. Cassava varieties contain prussic acid (hydrocyanide), which has to be removed before cooking!

Rainforest Canopy Walkway R.05

Take to the trees. Our Walkway is fully accessible to wheelchairs and pushchairs.

People and the forest

The Baka people from the rainforests of the Cameroon, the Congo basin and Gabon are deeply connected to nature. The forest is their mother, father and guardian, providing their food, medicines and shelter. They have hunted and gathered, led a very low-impact life and sung and played their way through life for thousands of years. You can listen to their music in their basecamp. Today their way of life, superb listening skills, deep forest knowledge and the forest itself are under threat.

Up on the Walkway discover what canopy scientists get up to and spot their IKOS pod – an authentic aerial campsite. Across the Biome spot our Canopy Bubble, a genuine piece of research equipment used by scientists to study the rainforest canopy. Our green team use ours to study our canopy and to prune the parts that others cannot reach.

'Rainforest peoples are the original tropical ecologists. We still have much to learn from them if we are to manage rainforest ecosystems in a sustainable manner... The recording and preservation of this indigenous knowledge is vital to our future survival.'

Professor Sir Ghillean Prance, FRS

Funding and phasing

Thank you to the Garfield Weston Foundation, the Wolfson Foundation, donors to the Eddie George Memorial Appeal and donations from other organisations, individuals, visitors and Friends who made this first phase possible. We are currently fundraising for the next phase, where we hope to make weather and explore climate.
edenproject.com/walkway

'The Rainforest conservation projects which are successful are those which work with the local indigenous people.' Andrew Mitchell, globalcanopy.org

Plants and the forest Look out for the stories about the tall tremendous trees as you walk towards the Nest platform.

The Nest platform Plants eat, drink, reproduce and protect themselves from danger – without moving. The Biodiversity Chandelier *(left)* explores nature's designs which have produced forms that fit their function: from fiercely protective prickles to extraordinary pollination mechanisms.

Challenges Forests are cleared for agriculture, mining, development and timber. 12–20% of carbon emissions (which contribute to climate change) come from deforestation. Over 100 rainforest species may be lost every day. To ensure our future survival we need to help the forests to survive.

Solutions Rainforests can regrow or be replanted and managed sustainably for the future.

- **Share** what you discover about how forests keep us alive.
- **Support** charities and organisations working to save the forest.
- **Shop** for products which look after the forest (eg. FSC, Rainforest Alliance) and avoid ones that don't (not just oil palm; forests are often felled to grow soya and meat).
- **Write** letters on rainforest issues to politicians.
- **Volunteer** for a rainforest charity.

Welcome to crops and cultivation R.07

Beyond the arch, find the plants that produce things we use: rubber, cocoa, chocolate, bananas. It's all a matter of balance between conserving the wild and cropping the land.

Growing with the forest R.08

'Slash and burn' is a common practice used by desperate peasant farmers. Alley-cropping, where crops are grown between rows of Inga trees, is a new alternative. This agro-forestry system is good for the forest and the people. The trees, like their relations peas and beans, contain special root bacteria which make nitrogen fertiliser from the air. The trees also provide shade, fruits (ice-cream bean) and can be cut back and used as a weed-suppressing mulch which rots down to make compost. (NB: Not all legumes – pea and bean trees – have edible fruits; some are poisonous.)

Regrowing the forest R.09

Rainforests can regrow. Archaeological evidence shows that over time 70% of the Amazon has been regenerated. Even so, it can be given a helping hand. Replanting pioneer trees quickly creates canopy cover, suppresses weeds, attracts animals that bring in seeds and nurtures timber tree species. Eden works on and with projects that help.

Rubber R.10

Photo: John Lennon

Rubber trees, *Hevea brasiliensis*, grow wild in the South American Amazon rainforest and have been tapped for rubber for boots and balls for centuries. However, growing demand for car tyres in the 20th century stimulated the plantation industry in Asia, where cultivated trees replaced rainforest. Demand for natural rubber is still high. Condoms, rubber gloves, shoe soles and many other products still use natural rubber.

How can we help save the rainforest, harvest important resources and enable the rainforest peoples to make a decent living?

WWF and Sky Rainforest Rescue are working with the Acre State Government in Brazil to help save one billion trees and make the forest worth

WORKING TOGETHER TO HELP SAVE 1 BILLION TREES

more alive than dead. Find out about one aspect of the project, working with local rubber-tapping communities to help make rubber tapping economically viable for local farmers, here at Eden. For more information visit **sky.com/rainforestrescue**

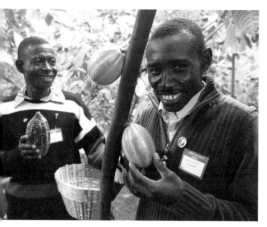

Cocoa and chocolate R.11

Cocoa originated in South America. Today it is grown by around 2.5 million farmers, mainly on West African smallholdings. The UK chocolate industry supports schemes like Fairtrade.

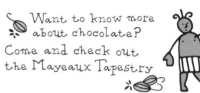

Want to know more about chocolate? Come and check out the Mayeaux Tapestry

Ghanaian cocoa farmers from the Kuapa Kokoo Co-operative admiring Eden's cocoa crop

The Mayeaux Tapestry in the Rainforest Biome takes you through the chocolate timeline.

AZTECS CONQUERED

COCOA GOES TO SPAIN

The Latin name for cocoa, *Theobroma*, means 'food of the gods'. Our chocolate 'extra-ordinary' ice-cream is made with fairly traded 'fino de aroma' Colombian cocoa: top-notch, said to be the best in the world.

Scientists are crossing West African cocoa trees with their wild South American ancestors (we've some growing by the bottom path) to create disease-resistant trees which means growers can use fewer chemicals and plant less on new land.

Stories from the rainforest R.12

Looks at what you can do to make a difference (see p.27).

Palms R.13

Many palms are used in the tropics, for food, fuel, walls, thatch, ropes, boats, sago, sugar, cooking oil... However, one palm has become a global commodity. Oil palm produces 'vegetable oil', found in nearly half of bestselling supermarket lines, even cleaning products and cosmetics. Orangutans' habitats are felled for oil palm plantations. We don't use palm oil in our Cornish pasties (yes, even pasties sometimes contain palm oil). Global supply chases demand, and plantations march into the rainforest. The Roundtable on Sustainable Palm Oil works on sustainable production. **rspo.org**

Bananas and Mangoes R.14

Bananas Over 85% of the bananas grown in the tropics stay there, a staple diet for millions. Different varieties provide local favourites for savoury or sweet dishes, juice, wine and beer. The bananas that reach our shores are generally Cavendish types from large plantations (such as those in Latin America, usually owned by large companies) or from smallholdings (such as those in the Caribbean, usually owned by local farmers). Organic and/or fairly traded bananas are available in shops; your wallet is your weapon. Panama disease has blighted Cavendish crops worldwide, so growers are trying new varieties – and so are we.

Mangoes For us a delicious treat, for some a promising export crop for developing countries and for others a vital famine food.

Sugar R.15

Sugar is made from tropical sugar cane (and temperate sugar beet). In the 1300s we each used around a teaspoon a year. Today it's around 35kg, and stories of diabetes, obesity and poor teeth abound. Sugar cane is also used for ethanol production. According to the industry, this doesn't get caught in the food or fuel debate (unlike maize) and doesn't displace rainforest. Bagasse, the waste product, can be burnt to generate electricity. Over 7m people are employed worldwide in the sugar industry, many in developing countries. Fairtrade and organic sugar are also on the up; the sugar used at Eden is fairly traded.

Rice R.16

Rice is the seed of one of the most widely grown grasses in the world. Farmers grow it to eat and sell, some to us. Scientists are working on rice breeding programmes to increase yields to feed the growing population and are also working in partnership with poor farmers, exploring how to grow rice in different and difficult environments.

Tropical fruits R.17

Baobab We serve refreshing baobab smoothies here when possible. The baobab tree, from Africa, is called the tree of life. It can provide shelter, clothing and water as well as food.

Our baobab fruit comes through PhytoTrade Africa and money raised helps support the harvesters in Southern Africa. Our baobab bar is surrounded by an array of tropical fruits, including soursop, rambutan and the unusual jaboticaba tree.

Bamboo R.18

Bamboo is used by half the world's people to make homes, furniture, food, fuel, music, medicine, scaffolding and suspension bridges. Its hollow tubes are strong but light. Within its tissues short, tough fibres sit in a resilient matrix: nature's fibreglass.

Coffee R.19

Coffee is big business. The beans grow inside coffee cherries *(right)* which ripen at different times, making picking tricky. Eden uses Direct Trade coffee from specific farms in El Salvador, Guatemala and Honduras, whose farmers care for their workers and the environment. The coffee is shade-grown under diverse trees which helps conserve biodiversity. It is sourced for us – direct – by the Cornish company Origin: meaning fewer links in the coffee journey chain. They roast it in the most energy-efficient roasters too. Keep your eye out for Direct Trade. It's happening in coffee – where next?

Nuts and spices R.20

Today spices are cheap. In the past they were worth their weight in gold and shaped the world as we know it. Explore the stories on the spice boat and see if you can solve its riddles.

Nutmeg Though nutmeg was thought to cure the bubonic plague, it was along the spice route from Central Asia that the Black Death first travelled to Europe in the mid-1300s.

Ginger Has many relations: turmeric, cardamom, torch ginger, galangal, which are used for flavourings, starch production, antiseptics and in cultural ceremonies. Some gingers are NTFPs (non-timber forest products), harvested from the rainforest without harming the trees or environment. Good for plants, good for people.

Cashews Why are cashews *(middle right)* so expensive? Roasting, shelling and cleaning the nuts is laborious and the shells contain highly corrosive cashew-nut shell liquor (CNSL). Traditionally used to treat ringworm, CNSL is now sometimes used in heatproof enamels and brake pads.

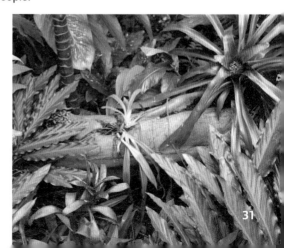

Secrets of the rainforest R.21

Come and enjoy the beauty of canopy plants like these bromeliads.

31

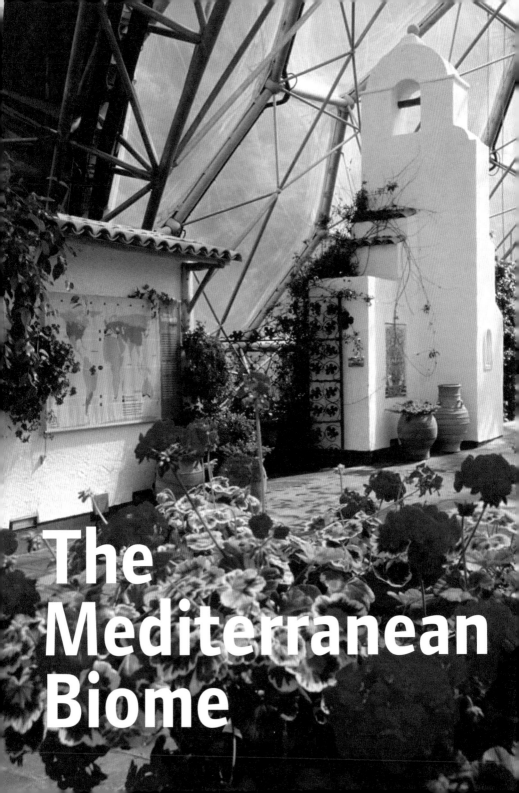

The Mediterranean Biome

The Mediterranean Biome

Salutare! Enter all – The Lands of the Warm Temperate Regions
Journey through:
The Mediterranean's Paradise
South Africa's Garden
California's Horn of Plenty
Born of Sister Fire and Brother Drought

Immerse yourself in Culture's Cradle
Taste history, olives, citrus and wines
In the world's kitchen gardens
Born of Water and Mankind

Welcome to the Mediterranean Biome M.01

Mediterranean-type climates with their hot, dry summers and cool, wet winters are located 30–40°N or S latitude on the western sides of continents. They are within the Warm Temperate climate zone.

In this Biome we invite you to meander through the wild landscapes of the Mediterranean, South Africa and California. Wild? Through history many of these landscapes have been shaped by human cultures.

The native plants in all these regions have to cope with drought and poor, thin soils. Some have small, grey, hairy leaves, some make protective oils, some are spiny, evergreen and/or waxy. This may help to reduce water loss and make the plants less appetising to predators.

The plants are tough but their environments are fragile: intensive grazing erodes soils, imported plants threaten native species, land is developed and precious water is used to serve the needs of crops and people, many of whom are occasional visitors. Big pressure on small lands.

Crops? The addition of water and fertilisers to these sunny regions has created massive kitchen gardens for vegetables, vines, fruits and flowers. Take a look round. You'll find many familiar products come from these places: wine, olive oil, perfumes, lemonade.

On your journey, look out for Dionysus, the great bronze bull. He stands centre field, straddled between the wild and the cultivated lands. As he discovered (to his peril), it's all a matter of balance. It's in our gift to leave the world better than we found it.

The Mediterranean Basin M.02

Through the gates to your left, a typical Mediterranean garden. Back on the main, lower route (no steps), the 'Liquid Gold' mosaic path created by Elaine Goodwin *(right)* celebrates the tradition of olive oil as a symbol of life and divinity. Look for the subtle dove images – one for each Mediterranean nation.

The Mediterranean landscape is mainly man-made, cleared for crops over many thousands of years, including the olives and vines that helped shape this region's civilisation. The ancient terraced olive groves support more animal species than would a pine forest. Today many people leave their mountain farms seeking work on the coast, although city dwellers are beginning to return to smallholdings. Buying traditional foods and natural products, seeking out quality and taste, farm holidays: all can help conserve these fragile environments and communities.

Past the bell tower, the upper stepped route takes you through Maquis and Garrigue to the viewing point. The French underground movement in World War II was called the Maquis because they hid in this hilly landscape of prickly oak, juniper and broom, a habitat that contains unique plants, insects and reptiles, but can get overlooked, having no spectacular birds or mammals.

South Africa M.03

The Cape Floral Kingdom has over 1,400 rare or endangered plant species. Fynbos, with around 7,000 species (5,000 unique to this area), covers 80% of this kingdom.

'*Fain-boss*', Afrikaans for 'fine bush', refers to the evergreen, fire-prone shrubs in this nutrient-poor soil. Plants include rush-like restioids, shrubby heathers and proteoids, with their stunning feather-like blooms. Formed millions of years ago from the ashes of drought-stressed forests, the Fynbos has been fire-managed for conservation since the 1960s; The seeds of the Protea *(right)* need exposure to smoke to germinate. The Fynbos is threatened by agricultural and urban development, uncontrolled fire and invasive alien tree species.

Little Karoo In this semi-arid valley behind the southern coastal mountain range, the land bakes to 50°C in summer, freezes in winter and suffers severe droughts. Today much of the valley is irrigated for crops, but the surrounding hills house ice plants, aloes and types of daisy.

Namaqualand This red desert, 250 miles north of Cape Town, blooms into a multi-coloured carpet after winter rain. Different species germinate in different years, depending on when the rains come, taking it in turns to share the scarce water. Descendants of these wild plants, pelargoniums and daisies, are garden favourites.

California M.04

California has vast landscapes and a huge diversity of plants. Ceanothus and Californian poppies, familiar garden plants, grow wild here. The spiky chaparral, with its less familiar buck bush, toyon and scrub oak (the 'chaparro'), gave its name to chaparreros, or 'chaps', worn by cowboys to protect their legs. Chaparral, grassland and the open oak forests were the results of thousands of years of controlled burning by Native Americans. California once had a rich natural harvest that was cultivated gently and sustainably by the indigenous people. Today water is so valuable that environmental activists take out court orders to make farmers leave minimum flows in rivers.

The state's high consumption brings social and environmental costs, putting it at the forefront of climate change. On the other hand, the region is also the birthplace of innovative new technology and home to some of today's most environmentally conscious people. The catalytic converter started life here and 2010 saw the first legislation to give polluting companies such as utilities and refineries financial incentives to emit fewer greenhouse gases.

Welcome to crops and cultivation M.05

Many of our crop exhibits are seasonal, so please expect changes from time to time. Producing crops in the Mediterranean regions is an intensive industry using fertiliser, water, sprays and often immigrant labour. Pressure is mounting to move to low-input, energy-efficient, diversified farming. Water is becoming increasingly scarce; many aquifers have more water extracted from them than they receive. Technologies are being developed to reduce usage and explore creating fresh water from sea water and waste water.

Cork M.06

Agriculture and conservation work hand in hand in the bio-diverse cork oak wood pastures. Cork bark is harvested and Iberian pigs, which feed on the acorns, help maintain the plant diversity and provide high-value ham. These trees, unlike others, don't die when their bark is cut off, so buying cork products supports these environments. Currently supply is outstripping demand. Organisations such as WWF, the RSPB and the Portuguese Cork Association work to conserve these wood pastures. Buying wine (and champagne!) with real corks helps, but cork has many other properties and uses. It can cope with extreme temperatures, so can be used as engine gaskets, for example. Maybe new industrial applications could help save these landscapes?

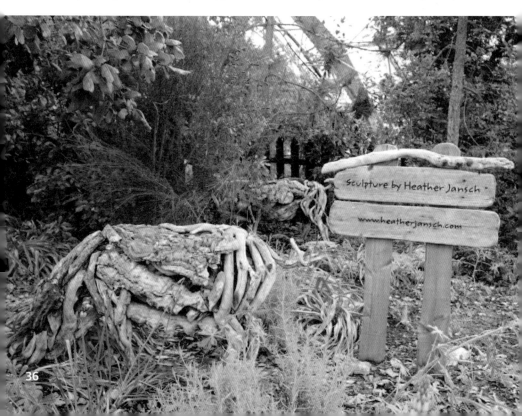

Sculpture by Heather Jansch
www.heatherjansch.com

The Mediterranean orchard M.07

Kiwis, peaches and loquats from China, almonds and apricots from Iran and Feijoa from Brazil have moved to the Mediterranean and California to soak up the sun and the water from the irrigation lines.

Seasonal crops M.07/M.08/M.09

Depending on the time of year you'll find chillies and peppers, tobacco, sunflowers, grains, pulses (peas and beans) and a range of growing systems.

Chillies   There are dozens of varieties, from mild to unbearable. Chilli heat is measured in Scoville Heat Units, and the hottest variety found so far is rated at 2,000,000 SHU, whereas your basic supermarket green chilli comes in at 1,500! Chillies *(right)* and sweet peppers are easy to grow – you'll find seeds and plants in the Eden shop.

Citrus M.10

The citrus family is fond of breeding. Clementines are a cross between mandarins and bitter Seville oranges, and tangelos the offspring of tangerines and grapefruits. Citrus fruits provide vitamin C and nutraceuticals (more on these in The Core Café in the Core). Citrus oils are used in flavourings, cleaning products, perfume, anti-bacterial agents, CFC substitutes and even fuel.

Plants for cut flowers M.12

85% of our cut flowers are imported, causing environmental and social challenges but also potential for jobs and a step out of poverty. Check out the label. Seasonal blooms with low 'flower miles' mean you can say it with sustainable flowers!
edenproject.com/shop

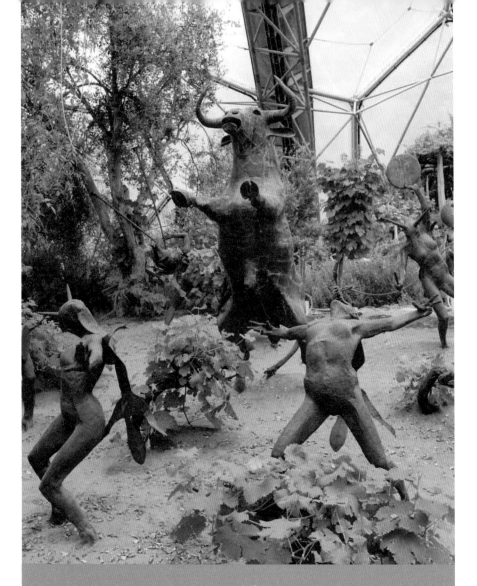

Dionysus – a question of balance

This potent nature god, here depicted as a bull, was associated with horticulture, fertility, wine, festivities, intoxication, illusion and also destruction. Dionysus started out with good intentions as the god of vegetation. However, things changed when he went from growing the vine to drinking its fermented juices ... party time! The land, like Dionysus, has changed. Here he stands, straddled between the ancient landscapes and the irrigated lands of intensive agriculture.

It's possible to go too far. It's possible to regain the balance. People can change things for the better. Tim Shaw created this wild Bacchanal where dancing Maenads mirroring the shapes of the vines surround their god, Bacchus (aka Dionysus).

Grape vines M.11

Grapes were one of the first cultivated fruits and today are the most widely planted fruit crop worldwide. Our long-term relationship stemmed from our ability to preserve them, by drying and far more consequential by turning them into an alcoholic drink.

Olives M.13

Once olive oil provided light for lamps and anointed the brave. Now used mostly in the kitchen, it is thought to reduce cholesterol levels and deter heart disease. Production is up but the squeeze is on to reduce chemical inputs. There is as much variation in taste and character in olive oil as there is in wine.

The Med Terrace and vegetable, herb and fruit garden M.14

The classic Mediterranean diet is associated with good health and long life. The diet is based around:

· fresh vegetables (including greens, salads and legumes)
· fruits and herbs
· nuts and cereals
· olive oil (monounsaturated fat)
· a bit of fish, poultry and dairy (yogurt or cheese)
· small amounts of red meat (low intake of saturated fats)
· a little alcohol (usually wine with a meal)

Is it just the food or is it also getting together with friends and family to relax and chat that does you good? Savour the flavour in the Med Cafe and watch your food growing around you.

Artichokes Full of antioxidants, aid digestion, provide roughage and are used by some as a hangover cure. They are also said to lower bad cholesterol and to be good for the liver.

Tomatoes When tomatoes were first introduced, Europeans thought the bright fruits were poisonous so grew them as ornamentals and used their perfumed leaves to treat skin complaints. Now we know them as a good source of vitamins A, E, C and antioxidants.

Eden Live – Seasonal Events Programme

The seasonal programme for 2014/15

Eden Live's events programme provides a different Eden every time you visit. There's something for all the family. For dates and the latest programme visit **edenproject.com**

Spring

Early spring: A celebration of all things Cornish including our annual World Pasty Championships.

Easter holidays: Eden's Chocolate Festival, with chocolate, chocolate – and more chocolate!

May Day Bank Holiday weekend: The Gruffalo's 15th Birthday.

May half-term week: Storytelling Festival.

Summer

Early summer: A range of exhibitions and the Sessions.

Summer holidays: Wild summer days (and evenings). Family activities, barbecues and a special rather large treat or two.

Autumn

Global Harvest: The world's bounty – celebrate it, preserve it, eat and drink it. Includes our annual beer festival.

October half-term: Halloweden. All things spooky, with, of course, our Little Monsters Ball.

Winter

Early winter: Enchanted Eden.

Christmas at Eden: music, processions, workshops, and Father Christmas. A time to give thanks for the things we give each other and the natural resources that nurture us.

February half-term: a programme of delights for all ages.

Ticketed events

Eden Sessions (**edensessions.com** for bands and full details).

Party time and special treats such as meeting Father Christmas: some for adults, some for all and some just for the kids (**edenproject.com**).

We also run a range of workshops and specialist days, such as 'be a gardener for the day' and tours, including our ever-popular chilli and chocolate tour.

Contact the **boxoffice@edenproject.com** or ring 01726 811972 for details or to register interest.

Eden – the back story

The Eden Project, established as one of the Landmark Millennium Projects to mark the year 2000 in the UK, is an international visitor destination featuring spectacular planting and architecture in a spectacular setting.

We're an educational charity, celebrating our connections and dependencies on plants and on each other. We all know that the 21st century brings many challenges: food security, moving and rising populations, plant and animal extinctions, increasing energy costs, economic shifts – all cranked up by climate change.

What to do? Sit and weep or do something about it? Eden regenerated this china clay pit as a symbol of transformative change, to demonstrate what people can do when they collaborate and put their minds to something. The world's challenges will demand the best of all of us: our creativity, ingenuity, understanding, science, technology, enterprise, humanity and most of all our ability to work together as healthy communities and resilient societies. It's all possible: humans can be pretty resourceful when they are asked to raise their game.

Our exhibits and events tell many of the changing stories of plants and people. Eden also works on and shares examples of many practical projects both on our doorstep and worldwide that explore new ways of living in the 21st century.

> 'The future is ours to invent. Let's create a world we want to live in.'
> Dr Tony Kendle, Creative Director, Eden Regeneration Ltd

Your entrance fees and the money you spend during your visit go to support both the operation of the site and Eden's public and formal education programmes and projects.

Eden is also a social enterprise, doing business to give the greatest possible ben to the widest number of people and show that improving the environment and livelihoods and building stronger communities can work hand in hand. Since 2001 Eden's 13m+ visitors have helped us put well over a billion pounds into the regional economy through year-round trade with local suppliers and businesses.

2000

2014

Regeneration and the art of the possible

The beginning of the story:

'Around the late 1990s a small group of people gathered in pubs, hotels and offices to talk about an idea – to create a place like nothing anyone had ever seen before; a place that explored our place in nature, a place that demonstrated what could be done if people who wanted to make a difference got together. It was ridiculous to imagine it was possible and that hundreds of people trained to say no could be persuaded to say yes. But the greybeards had a brilliant plan: ask the youngsters to do it – they don't know it can't be done.' Tim Smit, *Eden*

While Tim Smit (now Sir Tim, Executive Chairman, Eden Regeneration Ltd and co-founder of the Eden Project) was restoring the Lost Gardens of Heligan he realised that plants could be made far more interesting by weaving human stories around them, tales of adventure, emotion and derring-do. There was a big story to be told: plants that changed the world. A summer sunset on a china clay tip conjured thoughts of ancient civilizations in volcanic craters, and of putting the largest greenhouses in the world in a huge hole. Why not? We bought an exhausted, steep-sided clay pit 60 metres deep *(below)*, the area of 35 football pitches, with no soil, 15 metres below the water table, and gave it life: a huge diversity of plants we use every day but often don't get to see, planted in soil made from 'waste' materials, watered by the rain, in giant conservatories and buildings that drew inspiration from nature.

> 'Never underestimate the power of a small group of people to change the world. In fact, it is the only way it ever has.' Margaret Mead

Making it happen...

In 1994 Restormel, our local Borough Council at the time, took a leap of faith and put up the first £25,000, so giving the story a beginning.

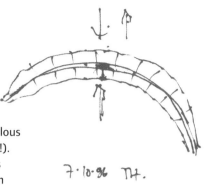

A year on, Grimshaws the architects took the baton from Cornish architect Jonathan Ball (co-founder of the Project) and designed our fabulous buildings (at risk, though we paid them in the end!). The McAlpine Joint Venture worked for 18 months without payment or contract and then loaned Eden a significant sum only to be repaid if the Project was successful. This risk-sharing broke down the traditional barriers between designers and

The first Biome sketch, 1996, in the pub, on the proverbial napkin.

contractors and created a team dedicated to one vision. Why did they do this? Because they wanted to change something and because they wanted to say, 'I'm glad I did,' rather than, 'I wish I had.'

Sound simple? Not really. We were turned down by the Millennium Commission the first time we applied, and many left good jobs before we had raised a bean – or found a site. When our reworked bid secured £37.5m from the MC (huge thanks, MC), we had to match it. For the next 5 years a small team worked tirelessly (mainly in a shed) to turn the idea into a plan and then into reality. Money was raised, fledgling teams grew thousands of plants, mapped them on to the site, started planning the stories … We recruited a team to run the place and made sure that as well as having a good idea and a fabulous theatre we had the ability to operate it. The Visitor Centre opened in 2000 so the public could watch the construction and share the adventure. The whole site opened on 17 March 2001. For more, read Tim Smit's *Eden* and visit **edenproject.com**.

The recipe for Eden

- Take an exhausted, steep-sided clay pit 60m deep, the area of 35 football pitches, with no soil, 15 metres below the water table.
- Carve the pit into a flat-bottomed bowl and landscape the sides.
- Mix and add 83,000 tonnes of soil made from recycled waste.
- Add superb architecture that draws inspiration from nature to remind us of human potential.
- Colonise with a huge diversity of plants, many that we use every day (but don't often get to see).
- Harvest the water draining into the pit and use it to irrigate our plants (and flush the loos!).
- Season with people from all walks of life.
- Spring 2000, open for a preview of the making.
- Spring 2001, open and serve.

Massive sandpit to global garden

To make the pit suited to people rather than mountain goats 17 metres was sliced off the top and put in the bottom. 1.8 million tonnes were shifted in 6 months. Dodgy slopes were shaved to a safe angle and terraces created. 2,000 rock anchors (some 11 metres long), stabilised the pit sides. A plant seed soup was sprayed on the slopes to knit the surface.

The answer lies in the soil

83,000 tonnes of soil was made. Minerals came from mine waste (sand from Imerys china clay and clay from WBB Devon Clays Ltd). In the Biomes, composted bark provided long-lived organic matter. The Rainforest Biome plants needed a rich organic soil that could hold water and nutrients, while the slower growers in the drier Mediterranean Biome used a sandier mix. A nutrient-free mix was used in South African Fynbos, where fertile soil is toxic to some native plants. Outdoors, we used composted domestic green wastes. Worms were added to help dig and fertilise.

The Biomes: building the world's largest conservatories

Building 'lean-to greenhouses' on uneven surfaces is tricky. 'Bubbles' were used because they can settle on any shaped surface.

Overall design

Two-layer, curved space frame, 'the hex-tri-hex', with an outer layer of hexagons (the largest 11 metres across), plus the odd pentagon, and an inner layer of hexagons and triangles bolted together. The steelwork weighs only slightly more than the air contained by the Biomes. They are more likely to blow away than down, so are tied into the foundations with ground anchors (giant tent pegs).

Transparent foil 'windows'

Ethylenetetrafluoroethylenecopolymer (ETFE): three layers, inflated 2-metre-deep pillows, lifespan over 25 years, transmit UV light, non-stick, self-cleaning. They weigh less than 1% of the equivalent area of glass, but can take the weight of a car. We got into the *Guinness Book of Records* for using the most scaffolding, 230 miles of it – sorry to anyone who was needing some that year.

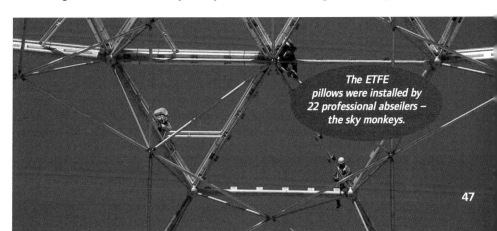

The ETFE pillows were installed by 22 professional abseilers – the sky monkeys.

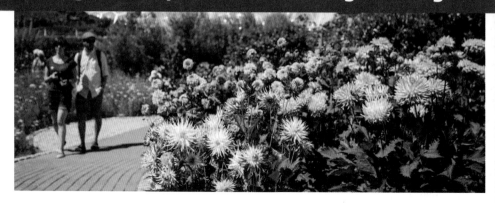

Bring on the plants – extreme gardening

Our Green Team often plant on near-vertical banks; have planted millions of plants of around 5,000 types; plant over half a million bulbs every autumn; plant around 60,000 new plants annually; start at 7.30 every day to prune and water before you arrive; do 50 hours weeding a week in the summer; remove about 25m³ of green waste from the site every week; recycle this material to make over 120 tonnes of compost a year.

Plants Many are grown from seed in our nursery, some come from botanic gardens, research stations and supporters, mostly in Europe and the UK. We keep a record of every plant on site. Pollination: some plants are insect-pollinated, some wind-pollinated, some paintbrush-pollinated! We do this when we need the flowers to produce seeds.

Pruning Rainforest trees are pruned by abseilers, from cherry picker and Canopy Bubble.

Pest and disease control Our rigorous healthcare programme starts with isolation houses at Eden's nursery to catch problems before they reach the site. On site our integrated pest management system uses cultural methods (removal of infested plant parts), 'soft' chemicals (soaps and oils) and biological control (bugs that eat bugs). Spot the little bamboo pots on pulley systems that give the bugs a ride to the treetops. Also eating their fill of pests are lizards, birds (e.g. Sulawesi White Eye, *cover*) and frogs (e.g. White's Tree Frog, *below*). Our UV lightboxes catch pests and monitor their numbers.

Climate In the covered Biomes it is monitored and controlled automatically. The main heating source is the sun; the back wall acts as a heat bank, releasing heat at night. Triple-'glazed' windows provide insulation, while air-handling units cool on hot days and heat on cool ones.

Rainforest Biome Kept between 18-35°C and up to 90% humidity.

Mediterranean Biome Drier; even in cooler periods the vents often open to reduce humidity and fungal problems.

Bring in the people

Since opening in 2000 we've developed exhibitions, events, workshops, courses, education programmes (for all), concerts, sustainable buildings, efficient operating, energy and waste systems and grown our team from 5 staff to 500, plus 163 volunteers. Teams report to the Board, who report to the Trust, who ensure the operation meets its charitable aims. Art, science, horticulture, education, management, retail, catering, philosophy, economics, design, construction, publishing, research, housekeeping, stewarding, guiding, fundraising, storytelling, marketing, media – between them the teams cover all these bases and more. We work with others whenever we can to discover new approaches and to share what we have learnt. Full details of Eden's structure can be found at **edenproject.com**.

We explore creative approaches to physical access and information sharing to ensure our work is accessible to all. See **sensorytrust.org.uk** for more.

Eden is a project, a living laboratory exploring new ways of doing things. The way we operate and the projects we run all test ways of living in the decades to come. We take people, the planet and profits with a purpose into account ('the triple bottom line' as it is often called). This begins with building an awareness of what we dare not lose and exploring what we need to work with to help create a viable society in the 21st century: massive social and environmental change, carbon reduction, energy security, food security, conservation, building communities that can cope.

We love stories

Story is a powerful means of captivating, providing insight, testing moral choices, painting possible futures, challenging and holding a mirror up in a way that is acceptable – personal and impersonal at the same time. Unless a culture has strong stories it loses its direction. Eden aspires to be a place where the stories of our future are created and told – the *Aesop's Fables* of the 21st century. Look out for our Narrators (Eden's storytellers and guides, *opposite* and *left*), who will share their stories with you.

Learning programmes

Our schools programme hosts over 45,000 young people a year. We aim to help provide context, purpose and meaning. You may spot young explorers in 'Rainforest Uncovered', reconnecting with science on the ultimate field trip. We also welcome over 10,000 further and 1,000 higher education students annually, covering a wide range of subjects including continuing professional development for teachers. We also run a range of leisure learning courses. See the website for details.

We're committed to reducing our carbon footprint, using resources efficiently, generating our own renewable resources and being self-sufficient in soil, water and energy where possible. Our tens of thousands of plants sequester carbon every day. We also operate a green travel plan. You can get involved too: see **edenproject.com**.

Energy efficiency
The Biomes' hexagons copy nature's honeycombs: maximum strength, minimum materials. All our buildings set high standards for good building design and process, and demonstrate the worth of natural materials and structures. Since 2008 we've reduced our emissions from gas use by 20%, and electricity by 18%. New control systems, boilers, lighting, etc (thanks partly to an interest-free loan from the Carbon Trust), should see a 20% reduction in CO_2 emissions in 2014.

Waste Neutral
We reduce, re-use and recycle our waste wherever possible (currently recycling 19 different waste streams) and we reinvest by purchasing items that are made from recycled materials. Since 2005 our in-vessel composter has turned 183 tonnes of food waste, 29 tonnes of green waste and 18 tonnes of cardboard waste into 119 tonnes of plant compost for use on-site.

Cleaner technologies
Photovoltaic panels installed on the Core roof, our workshops and warehouse buildings, together with a small wind turbine, generate clean electricity. Nearly half our water needs – averaging 20,000 bathfuls a day – are provided from harvested ground and rainwater on site by a subterranean drainage system. We use this resource to irrigate our plants and flush our loos.

> 'You never change things by fighting the existing reality. To change something, build a new model that makes the existing model obsolete.' R. Buckminster Fuller (1895–1983), architect, designer, visionary

Project: Geothermal

With EGS Energy, we've got planning permission for a deep geothermal plant to supply us with renewable heat and power, and export the excess electricity, enough for around 3,500 households. This new technology, if rolled out, has the potential to supply as much as 20% of the UK's electricity and all of its heating! More on this at **edenproject.com/geothermal**, and on our overall energy policy and action plan at **edenproject.com/sustainability**. EGS and Eden are in discussions with the government and commercial lenders to find the required funding.

Food and retail

From plant to plate: our sourcing policy means that the food we serve in our cafés reflects the stories we tell in our exhibits. It is responsibly sourced: fairly traded,

single-source, organic, seasonal and/or local and freshly made, often in front your eyes. We cater for vegetarians, vegans, meat-eaters, gluten-free diets. Check site for opening times of venues (some close in quieter periods).

We work with local growers, suppliers and companies to develop products for sale. Low food miles, seasonal and vegetarian dishes all help reduce greenhouse gas emissions. Fairtrade, organic and other certified products from further afield demonstrate that good trade is a vital part of sustainability. The products you find in our shop all have a story to tell and are sourced with the planet in mind.

Eden's
projects

Eden's projects

Eden was initially a response to our disconnection with nature. Today it is also a provocation to do things differently. We now work with many like-minded people we've met along the way. Here are just a few examples.

The Big Lunch

The Big Lunch is the UK's annual get-together for neighbours, providing the perfect recipe to have fun, feed community spirit and help to build stronger neighbourhoods. People are the key ingredient, with those taking part creating friendlier communities in which they start to share more, from conversation and ideas to skills and resources. And 5 years in, we know it really works, with 86% of people taking part this year saying it made them feel better about where they lived. At a Big Lunch small talk often leads to big talk, and together people start to tackle local issues; from reducing crime or feelings of isolation, to a whopping 90% reporting it brings different generations together. The Big Lunch is on the first Sunday in June every year. Have one! **thebiglunch.com**

Big Lunch Extras

We believe communities often hold the answers to what a better future looks like. Sometimes all they need is a little help along the way to unlock ideas, make things happen and get people involved. Big Lunch Extras builds on the success of the Big Lunch and supports individuals with the skills, confidence and motivation they need to create positive change where they live. **www.biglunchextras.com**

The Big Lunch and Big Lunch Extras are made possible by the Big Lottery Fund.

Green Foundation

We are living through a period of extraordinary transformation that will demand the very best of us. For businesses, we believe this means taking responsibility, doing things more sustainably and engaging successfully with staff and communities. We work with businesses who wish to stand to this challenge by assisting them in a variety of ways – from unlocking creativity and innovation, to sustainability, leadership and organisational culture. **www.greenfoundation.org.uk**

MSc Sustainability

Higher education can have a crucial role in shaping students into catalysts for change. We have formed an academic partnership with two like-minded organisations to deliver Eden's first ever MSc course – MSc Sustainability: Working for positive change. Our masters students go on a unique learning journey here at Eden and in Cambridge, preparing them to become successful change agents within the world of work. **www.mscsustainability.org**

Gardens for Life

Crossing communities, cultures and countries, Gardens for Life is a network of schools that explores the world through gardening and growing food. In Africa or India, being able to grow your own food can make a real difference to your prospects. This project works with schools and communities to feed minds and bodies, giving them essential skills for the future and helping ensure that everyone gets at least one square meal a day – using ingredients they've grown themselves. Free school meals help to ensure higher attendance rates and improve student grades, but if a whole community grows its own food everyone benefits. **edenproject.com/gardens-for-life**

Gardens for Life

Baobab

In 2012 fisherwoman Esther Kansaka *(left)* switched from trading fish to trading baobab. The fish trade barely kept the family from poverty but Esther and her husband were able to increase their income tenfold through the organic and sustainable trade in baobab fruit facilitated through TreeCrops – Malawi's baobab producer and member of PhytoTrade Africa, southern Africa's trade association for natural products.

The baobab we use in our products at Eden, rich in vitamins and minerals, is sustainably harvested and bought from rural harvester groups in Malawi. In addition, money from every sale of baobab powder goes to our friends at PhytoTrade Africa, who help support rural harvesters and producers across southern Africa. Project Baobab is funded by the Food Retail Industry Challenge Fund (FRICH) which supports African farmers by bringing their produce to European markets and shoppers.

Our journey continues, working with others, exploring new ways of doing things in education, in business and in communities.

Where has the money come from?

The Millennium Commission weighed in with £37.5m of lottery funding to single Eden out as the 'landmark' project of the far South West, and their subsequent contributions brought the total to just over £56m.

We hope we've delivered for them and for anyone who ever bought a lottery ticket. Other major sources of funding included the EU and Southwest Regional Development Agency (some £50m between them) and £20m of commercial loans. The balance was made up of other loans and some funds generated by Eden itself and reinvested back into the Project.

Maintaining a strong and diverse financial base is crucial to preserving the Eden Trust's independence and credibility. A full list of all our funders to date can be found at **edenproject.com/thankyous**. Thank you.

How much?

	£m
Buying a large and unusual site, car parks, roads and paths	16
Reshaping the ground to make it safe, dry and useful	8
A couple of decent greenhouses	26
40 acres of plants ... some tall	3
83,000 tonnes of manufactured soil to grow them in	2
A nursery to practise in and grow some unusual plants	1
Buildings for you and our team – fully equipped	22
Services to keep it all running	7
Paying the team up to opening	3
Exhibits to entertain you, walkways to keep you dry, a lift, a bridge	12
Advice on the things we couldn't do ourselves	12
Investments in our future like the Foundation building	9
A spectacular home for education – The Core	16
Warehouse, gatehouse, waste compound, Arena	4
Dreams cost money **Total**	**141**

Be involved

Eden is a charity and our work and successes are only possible thanks to the generosity of our donors, supporters and volunteers. **edenproject.com/support**

You can support our work in many ways

Visit us You're helping just by being here – all the profits from your visit go to the Eden Trust.

Gift Aid your admission fee This allows us to claim 25p back from the taxman on every pound you give.

Become an Eden Friend Eden Friends enjoy free entry to Eden, get exclusive access to our horticulture team, and play a vital role in supporting our charitable work.

For full details go to:
- **edenproject.com/friends**
- Ticketing Supervisors' desk in the Visitor Centre
- 01726 811932
- **friends@edenproject.com**

Make a donation edenproject.com/donations
The money we raise goes towards our work on public and formal education, research, conservation and sustainable futures.

Volunteer edenproject.com/careers/volunteering
Can you spare at least 6 hours a fortnight? Feel good, learn things, meet people – what's not to love? An ideal way to become involved in the daily work of the Project.

Register for our newsletter edenproject.com/e-newsletter

Useful numbers
General enquiries: 01726 811911 Box office: 01726 811972
Group bookings: 01726 811903 School bookings: 01726 811913

The Eden Project, Bodelva, St Austell, Cornwall PL24 2SG
The Eden Project is a registered charity no. 1093070

Contact us edenproject.com/contact-us

What can we do?

There's no shortage of top tips for a greener life: fitting energy-saving light-bulbs and so on. Useful? Yes and no.

They can trivialise the issues; saving the world isn't a matter of what goes in your basket, and it takes the heat off the big guys. But if we had to write our own Ten Top Tips (eleven, actually!), they'd go like this:

3. Learn about your life Is having 'stuff' bad? Not always: trade is not the same as consumption and can support livelihoods. Understand what sustains you and what you need to care about. Learning new talents and skills can help you get there.

1. Do stuff Don't waste it, turn it off, turn it down, do it less, do it local, do it yourself, recycle, swap, repair, share.

4. Increase your reach There's only so much you can do on your own. Try working with or through other organisations. Also don't forget that your wallet is your weapon. Make buying choices that help good things happen – worldwide.

2. Be hopeful Hope isn't just about crossing your fingers. Without it we could get cynical and frozen in despair. Hope is the fuel – but it only works if you do something.

5. Be angry at the things you can't change ... but think about who can change them. Demand that governments, companies and big organisations change with us and give us real choices.

9. Forgive yourself (and others)

Sustainable development will be a territory for endless exploration. Learn from mistakes. We make mistakes because we act, strive and aim high – and that is what makes us human.

6. Imagine different things The 21st century will be a time of transformation. Meet different people, explore different things, read different books, try out new ideas.

7. Give gifts and give thanks

Understand why we need each other. This is a time to support each other, to work together and build communities.

10. Have fun 'Living a sustainable life' isn't all about 'don't do this' sucking the joy out of living. Where is the adventure in that? There are worlds of possibility out there. Rich cultures, rich experiences, music, laughter, fun and just enjoying life more – foundations for a better future!

8. Get out more People can't care about what they don't understand and don't have some sense of connection to. So we need to get out and down in that dirt lest we forget how it keeps us alive. Play together, learn, explore and have adventures.

11. Be the change you wish to see in the world Gandhi's saying sounds like something from a hippie poster, but actually it was one of the greatest social insights of the 20th century. So, do everything positive you can, not because a list has told you to but because it's who you want to be.

First published 2001 by Eden Project Books, a division of Transworld Publishers

Fourteenth revised edition 2014

Text and design © the Eden Project/Transworld Publishers 2014

Text by Dr Jo Elworthy with assistance from the Eden team

Transworld Publishers, 61–63 Uxbridge Road, London W5 5SA,
a division of the Random House Group Ltd

booksattransworld.co.uk/eden

ISBN 978 1909513013

Editor: Mike Petty Design: Charlie Webster Printed in Great Britain

Cover photo by Seán Kelly

The Eden Project is owned by the Eden Trust, registered charity no. 1093070
and all monies raised go to further the charitable objectives.
Thank you for your support.

Eden Project, Bodelva, St Austell, Cornwall PL24 2SG

T: +44 (0)1726 811911 F: +44 (0)1726 811912

edenproject.com

Rainforest Biome

Tropical South America R.06

West Africa R.04 / R.05

Southeast Asia R.03

Tropical Islands R.02

Crops R.07 / R.08 / R.09 / R.10 / R.11

R.12 / R.13 / R.14 / R.15 / R.16 / R.17 / R.18 / R.19 / R.20 / R.21 / R.01

Size: 240m long, 110m wide, 50m high, 15,590m² **Plants:** Over 1,100 different species and cultivars **Temperature:** ranges from 18°C to 35°C **Comfort:** Seats and drinking water fountains throughout and a cool room in the West Africa area (R.04) for emergencies.

R.01 Welcome to the Rainforest Biome

R.02 Tropical islands

R.03 Southeast Asia

R.04 West Africa

R.05 Rainforest Canopy Walkway – phase 1

R.06 Tropical South America

R.07 Welcome to crops and cultivation

R.08 Growing with the forest

R.09 Regrowing the forest

R.10 Rubber

R.11 Cocoa and chocolate

R.12 Stories from the rainforest

R.13 Palms

R.14 Bananas and mangoes

R.15 Sugar

R.16 Rice

R.17 Tropical fruits

R.18 Bamboo

R.19 Coffee

R.20 Nuts and spices

R.21 Secrets of the rainforest